Flower

COLORING BOOK

_____

_____

Welcome to the world of flowers, where you can unleash your creativity and explore the beauty of nature with our flower coloring book!

This coloring book is a stunning collection of some of the most beautiful and vibrant flowers in the world. From delicate roses and elegant lilies to bright sunflowers and exotic hyacinths, you'll find a wide variety of flowers to color and bring to life.

But this coloring book is more than just a way to unwind and relax. Each flower illustration is accompanied by interesting facts and information about the flower's origins, symbolism, and cultural significance.

This coloring book is perfect for anyone who loves flowers, nature, or art. It makes a wonderful gift for yourself or for a loved one who could use a little bit of relaxation and inspiration. So grab your favorite coloring tools and get ready to immerse yourself in the beauty and wonder of the flower kingdom!

DELPHINIUM

Delphinium is derived from a
Greek word "delphis" which
means "dolphin." It is because the
shape of its closed flower buds
looks like the nose of a dolphin.

Delphiniums symbolize happiness
and goodwill. It is the perfect gift
to give to someone who
is born in July.

CALENDULA

Calendula is derived from a Latin word "calendae" which means "little calendar" or "little clock" because it flowers on every new moon. It is also known as marigold.

HYDRANGEA

Hydrangea is derived from Greek and it means "water pitcher" because the seed capsules of this flower resemble an ancient water pitcher.

The hydrangea represents grace, gratitude and beauty.

LAVENDER

LAVENDER IS DERIVED FROM "LAVARE" WHICH IS A LATIN WORD THAT MEANS "TO WASH." THIS MUST BE BECAUSE IT WAS OFTEN USED IN BATHS FOR ITS PLEASANT SMELL.

THE LAVENDER REPRESENTS DEVOTION, PURITY AND CALMNESS.

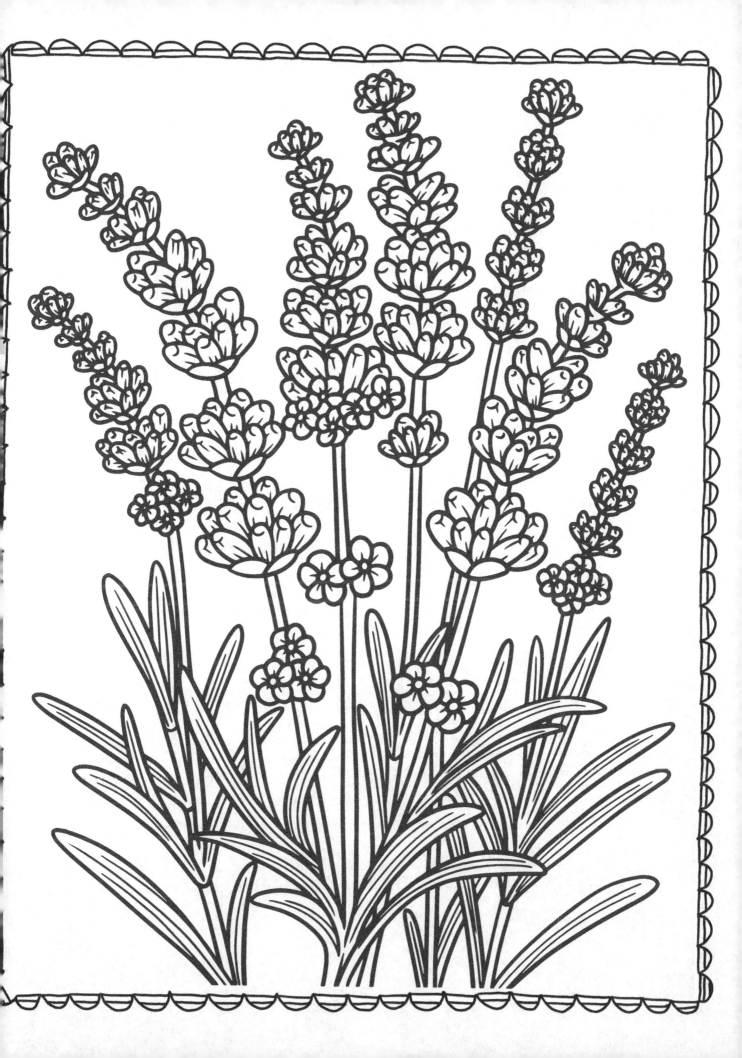

DAISY

Daisy is originated from "dægesege" which is an Old English word. It means "day's eye" because the petals of a daisy flower open at dawn and close at dusk.

Daisies symbolize new beginnings, joy, fun and innocence. It would be a great gift for a newborn baby and the baby's mother.

AMARYLLIS

Amaryllis comes from Greek and it means "to sparkle."

It is a very popular Christmas flower because of its rich, red color.

It symbolizes strength, pride and determination.

PROTEA

Protea is named after Greek God Proteus, son of Poseidon. Proteus had the power to transform its shape into anything he wished. This might be due to many different forms, colors and petal and leaf shapes of this beautiful flower.

It is one of the oldest flowers on Earth. It was blooming during the times of dinosaurs.

CAMELLIA

Camellia is named after a priest and botanist named George Kamel.

It symbolizes love, affection and devotion.

HYACINTH

Hyacinth gets his name from Greek mythology. The famous Greek historian and poet Homer used this word to name a plant that grew out of a young man's blood who was accidentally killed by Zephyr (Greek god of west wind).

It symbolizes jealousy and forgiveness.

JASMINE

Jasmine is originally a Persian word
which means "gift from God."

It is a fragrant flower that belongs
to the family of olives.

It is a symbol for love and beauty.

CYPRESS VINE

Cypress vine is a climbing plant that produces delicate, star-shaped flowers. They are are attractive to hummingbirds and butterflies.

These beautiful flowers symbolize Eternal Love.

BEGONIA

Begonias come in a variety of colors, including white, pink, yellow, orange, red, and even green. These cheerful flowers named after Michel Begon, a French patron of botany who lived in the 17th century.

Begonias are also considered symbols of mindfulness, growth, and renewal, and are often used in meditation and spiritual practices.

CHRYSANTHEMUM

The name "Chrysanthemum" is derived
from Greek. *Chryos* means "gold" and
anthemon means "flower". They are one of
the most popular fall flowers.

These beautiful flowers symbolize
friendship, happiness and well-being.

FORGET-ME-NOT

The name "forget-me-not" comes from an old German legend. This legend is about a knight who died trying to get flowers for his lover. His last words were: "forget me not!"

These beautiful flowers symbolize Endless Love.

HIBISCUS

Hibiscus is originally a Greek word which means "marshmallow plant."

Hibiscus flowers are very beautiful but most of them bloom only for a day.

Hibiscus flowers symbolize love, friendship and joy.

TULIP

Tulip is originally a Persian word which means "turban" because the flower looked very much like one.

You can find tulips in almost any color, they only bloom between 3-7 days in the spring.

Tulips are a symbol of perfect and deep love.

SUNFLOWER

Sunflower takes its name from Greek mythology. A beautiful girl fell in love with Apollo, the sun god. She would look at the sun all day long. Gods pitied her and turned her into a *SUNFLOWER*. This is why the sunflower follows the sun from dawn to dusk. And when the sun sets, it slowly turns to East waiting for the Sun to rise again.

These gorgeous flowers symbolize love, loyalty and adoration.

ORCHID

Orchids have the smallest seeds of all flowering plants. The seeds are so tiny that they can only be seen under a microscope.

Some orchid species bloom only for hours while some others can bloom for months.

They symbolize love, beauty and many children.

WATERLILY

Waterlilies are one of the most beautiful water plants. The leaves of waterlilies are coated in a waxy substance that repels water which allows them to stay dry and float on the water surface. Some waterlilies species are able to create their own heat in order to attract pollinators.

Waterlilies symbolize enlightenment and purity.

GARDENIA

Gardenias are named after Alexander Garden, a Scottish physician and naturalist who discovered the plant in Charleston, South Carolina in the 1700s. Gardenias were once considered a luxury item and were only available to the wealthy.

Gardenias symbolize purity, love, and spiritual awareness. In some cultures, gardenias are used to ward off evil spirits and bring good luck.

VIOLET

Violets are known for their heart-shaped leaves and delicate flowers. There are over 500 species of violets. Some species of violets are edible and can be used in cooking and baking.

They symbolize love and affection.

MAGNOLIA

The name "magnolia" was given in honor of French botanist Pierre Magnol. Magnolias have been around since the time of the dinosaurs. They are one of the oldest flowering plants on Earth.

Magnolia trees can grow up to 80 feet tall.

Magnolia flowers symbolize purity, nobility, and feminine beauty.

LAUREL

Laurel flowers are native to the Mediterranean region. Laurel flowers have small yellowish-green blossoms that appear in early spring. It has a beautiful smell and it is often used in perfumes.

Laurel flowers symbolize victory and wisdom.

LILAC

Lilacs are known for their sweet fragrance, which is often used in perfumes and candles. Lilacs bloom every spring, and their beautiful flowers only last for a few weeks. Lilacs are often used in bridal bouquets and wedding decorations.

The lilac flower symbolizes innocence and purity and joy of youth.

DAFFODIL

Daffodils are often associated with the story of Narcissus in Greek mythology, who fell in love with his own reflection and eventually turned into a flower.

Daffodils symbolize rebirth and new beginnings, making it a popular choice for Easter and other springtime celebrations.

Daffodils were traditionally thought to bring good luck and prosperity, and were sometimes planted near homes and businesses for this reason.

GERBERA

Gerbera is sometimes called the "happy flower" due to its bright and cheerful appearance.

Gerbera is a popular gift for Mother's Day, Valentine's Day, and other special occasions.

Gerbera is believed to bring good luck and positive energy into the home.

DAHLIA

The name "*Dahlia*" was given in honor of
Swedish botanist Andreas Dahl. Dahlia
flowers are known as the national flower of
Mexico.

Dahlia flowers symbolize dignity, elegance,
and forever-lasting love.

IRIS

Iris means rainbow in Greek. These beautiful flowers were named after Greek goddess Iris, who was the messenger of the gods and traveled on a rainbow, as these flowers come in a wide range of colors.

Irises were first cultivated in ancient Egypt and were considered a symbol of power and royalty.

CARNATION

The word *"Carnation"* comes from Latin and it means two things: "flower of the gods" and "flower of love."

The meaning of carnations varies by color. For example, red carnations are associated with love and admiration, while white carnations symbolize purity and luck.

MORNING GLORY

This beautiful flower is called "morning glory" because it opens in the morning and closes by late afternoon.

Morning glory is associated with happiness, good fortune, and love.

POPPY

People have been cultivating poppies for more than 5,000 years. They have been found in Egyptian tombs dating back thousands of years. In Greek mythology, the poppy flower is associated with Morpheus, the god of sleep and dreams.

Poppies symbolize sleep, peace, dreams and imagination.

PANSY

Pansy flowers bloom in a variety of colors including purple, yellow, white, blue and pink. They open up in the morning and close in the evening.

These colorful flowers symbolize all kinds of love: platonic love, romantic love or just general affection for somebody.

CROCUS

The name "crocus" comes from the Greek word "krokos," which means "saffron" that is because saffron, one of the most expensive spices in the world, is harvested from this flower.

These gorgeous flowers symbolize rebirth, innocence, joy, and new-beginnings.

ROSE

Roses are one of the most popular and widely cultivated flowers in the world, with thousands of different varieties. The thorns on a rose stem are actually modified leaves, and they help to protect the plant from predators.

Rose is a symbol of beauty and love.

LILY

Lily is one of the most popular flowers in the world. It is known for its beauty and its lovely smell. In ancient Rome, lilies were used in perfumes and cosmetics.

Lilies symbolize beauty, royalty, elegance, renewal and good luck.

LOTUS

Lotus seeds are unique because they are incredibly resistant, they can survive for hundreds of years.

The roots of the lotus flower are anchored in the mud, but the plant rises above the water to bloom. This is why this fascinating flowers symbolize the journey from darkness to light.

BULBOUS BUTTERCUP

The bulbous buttercup flower is known for its bright yellow petals and glossy green leaves. These flowers follow the sun.

The bulbous buttercup flower symbolize joy, youth, purity, happiness and friendship.

PEONY

Peonies are known to be attractive to butterflies and other pollinators, making them an important part of many ecosystems. Peonies can live for up to 100 years

These beautiful flowers symbolize symbolizing wealth, honor, and elegance.

APPLE BLOSSOM FLOWER

Apple blossoms are the flowers that bloom on apple trees. The flowers have a short blooming season, usually only lasting a few weeks in the spring. The flowers are white or pink and have a sweet, delicate fragrance.

Apple blossoms are a symbol of love and happiness in many cultures.

FREESIA

Freesia flowers come in a range of colors, including pink, red, yellow, white, and purple. Freesias have a sweet, delicate fragrance. They are named after the German botanist Friedrich Heinrich Theodor Freese who discovered the plant in the 19th century.

Freesia flowers symbolize innocence, friendship, and trust.

GLADIOLI

The word "gladioli" comes from the Latin word "gladius" which means sword, referring to the shape of the leaves. In ancient Rome, gladiolus flowers were associated with gladiatorial games and the victorious gladiators were showered with these flowers.

They symbolize wisdom, integrity, and strength.

POINSETTIA

Poinsettia was named after Joel Roberts Poinsett, the first U.S. ambassador to Mexico, who introduced the plant to the United States in the 1800s.

Poinsettias are often associated with Christmas because of their bright red and green colors, which symbolize the holiday season.

This flower is a symbol of hope and renewal, as they bloom during the winter months unlike many other plants.

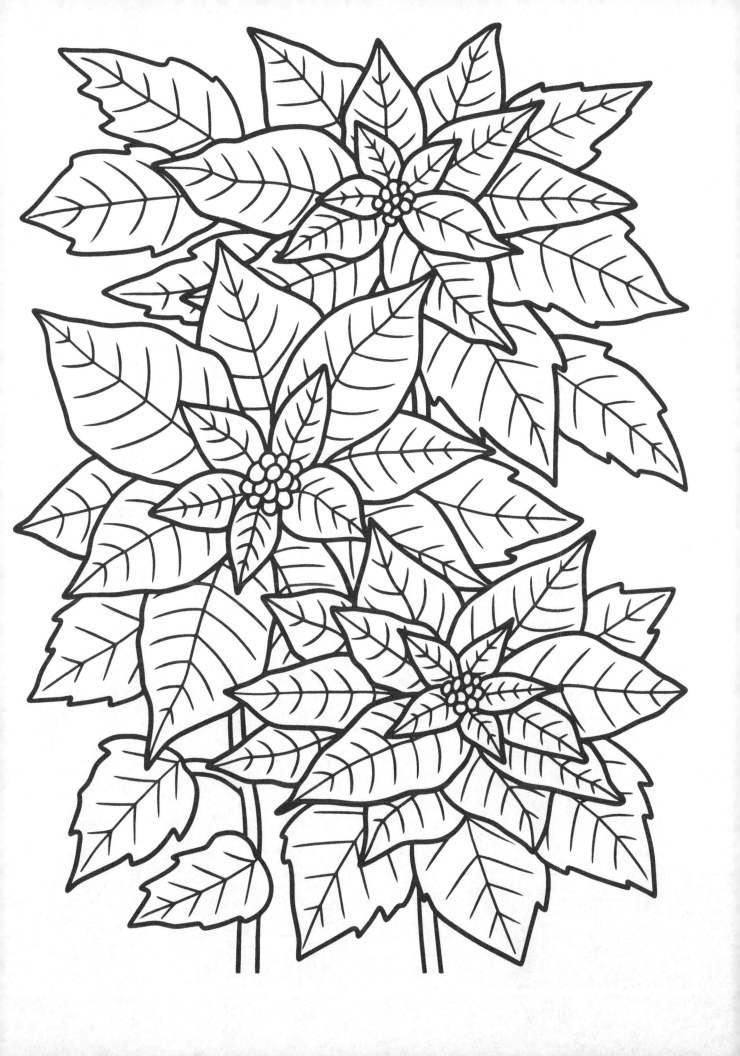

SNAP DRAGONS

The name "snapdragon" comes from the flower's resemblance to a dragon's head, which opens and closes its mouth when squeezed. Hummingbirds love these flowers.

Snapdragons symbolize deception and graciousness.

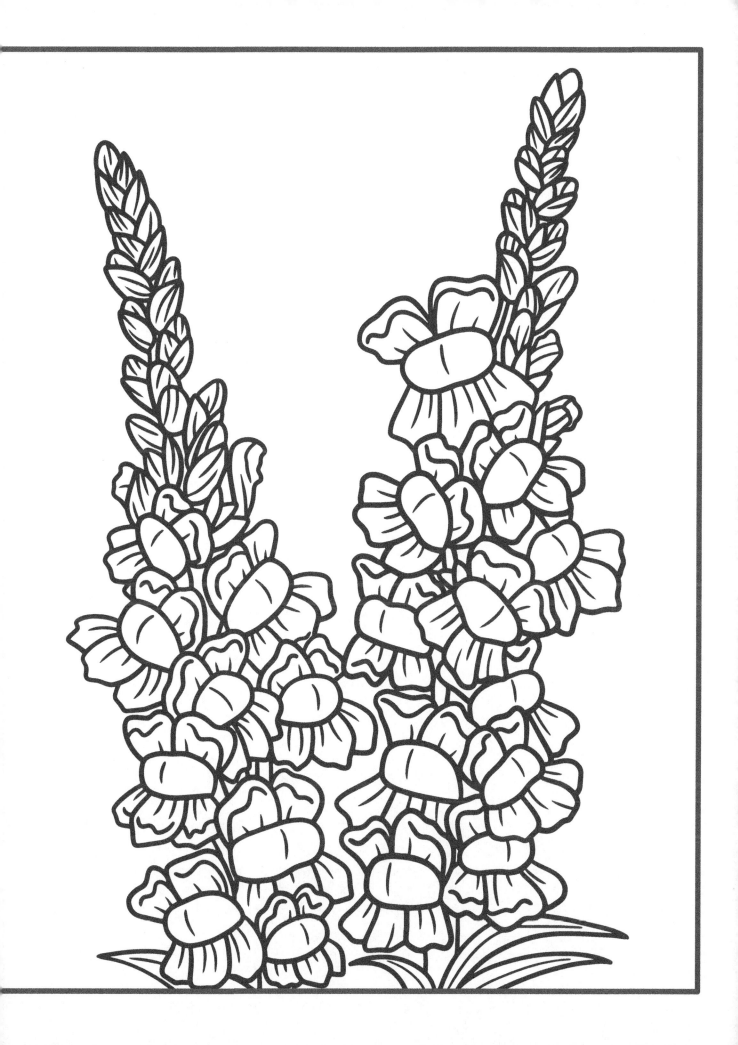

Made in the USA
Las Vegas, NV
06 August 2024

93461167R00050